To Ryker,

& hope you enjoy "Dayton Time"

Matt Green

EDGE BOOKS

DANGEROUS TIMES!
HISTORY'S MOST TROUBLED ERAS

by Matt Chandler

CAPSTONE PRESS
a capstone imprint

Edge Books are published by Capstone Press,
1710 Roe Crest Drive, North Mankato, Minnesota 56003
www.capstonepub.com

Copyright © 2014 by Capstone Press, a Capstone imprint. All rights reserved. No part of this publication may be reproduced in whole or in part, or stored in a retrieval system, or transmitted in any form or by any means, electronic, mechanical, photocopying, recording, or otherwise, without written permission of the publisher.

Library of Congress Cataloging-in-Publication Data
Chandler, Matt.
Dangerous Times!: History's Most Troubled Eras / by Matt Chandler.
pages cm.—(Edge books. Dangerous History)
Includes bibliographical references and index.
Summary: "Describes various eras of history, explaining why they were some of history's most troubled eras"—Provided by publisher.
Audience: Grade 4 to 6.
ISBN 978-1-4765-0126-0 (library binding)
ISBN 978-1-4765-3382-7 (eBook PDF)
1. History—Miscellanea—Juvenile literature. 2. Disasters—History—Juvenile literature. 3. War—History—Juvenile literature. 4. Violence—History—Juvenile literature. I. Title.
D24.C417 2014
904—dc23   2013018229

Editorial Credits
Jeni Wittrock, editor; Sarah Bennett, designer; Marcie Spence, media researcher; Jennifer Walker, production specialist

Photo Credits
Bridgeman Art Library: National Museum Wales, 19, Peter Newark American Pictures, 5, 11, Universal History Archives/UIG, 7; Getty Images: American Stock, 21, MPI, 13, Underwood Archives, 25, Universal History Archive, 1; Library of Congress, 17; North Wind Picture Archives, 15; Shutterstock: africa924, 27, Antonio Abrignani, 9, Nejron Photo, cover (bottom left and top right), PLRANG, cover (top left), solarseven, cover (bottom right), 23, Yes-Royalty Free, 28–29

Printed in the United States of America in Stevens Point, Wisconsin.
032013   007227WZF13

TABLE OF CONTENTS

Living in a Dangerous World.............4
The Middle Ages.......................6
Age of Exploration....................8
Colonial America.....................10
How the West Was Wild................12
Industrial Danger....................16
Death in the Great Depression........20
The Cold War and Fear................22
Danger in the 21st Century...........26

TIMELINE OF DANGEROUS ERAS............28
GLOSSARY..............................30
READ MORE.............................31
INTERNET SITES........................31
INDEX.................................32

LIVING IN A DANGEROUS WORLD

How safe is our world? Security systems and police forces make many people feel protected. If problems arise, help is only a cell phone call away. Thanks to modern medicine and **vaccinations**, once-deadly diseases are kept at bay.

Many dangers of past eras no longer threaten us today. But does that mean this era is any less dangerous? Not necessarily. It's true that few people die from grizzly bear attacks anymore. But on the other hand, in 2011, about 30,000 people died in car accidents in the United States alone. About 600,000 died of heart disease.

Would you rather face the black plague, a collapsing coal mine, or **terrorist** bombs? While no one is ever completely safe, some ages were definitely more deadly than others. Hold on tight as you travel through time to history's most troubled eras.

vaccination—a shot of medicine that protects people from a disease

terrorist—someone who uses threats and violence to frighten or harm people and to achieve a religious or political goal

In the 1800s, bear encounters were more common than they are today.

THE MIDDLE AGES

(400–1500)

The Middle Ages were filled with disease and warfare. Religious wars sent many people into battle. One violent series of conflicts between Christians and Muslims is known as the Crusades. These bloody battles claimed the lives of about 200,000 people.

With limited medical knowledge, many injuries and diseases had no real treatment. Outbreaks of the **bubonic plague** killed millions of people in the Middle Ages. Those who were infected got painful **boils**. Rashes covered their bodies and they coughed up blood. Most of the plague's victims died within a week of infection.

The many plagues and wars caused countless deaths. Rather than bury each body separately, survivors often dug mass graves to bury large groups of corpses. In some cases, the bodies were even used as weapons. Warriors catapulted corpses over enemies' fortresses like cannonballs.

bubonic plague—a fatal disease with painful swelling of the glands and a darkening of the skin

boil—a painful spot on the body that is swollen and is usually caused by an infection

FACT

The bubonic plague spread quickly because of the filthy living conditions. Without proper sanitation systems, the streets were filled with garbage and thousands of rats.

Bubonic plague victims were often buried in mass graves.

AGE OF EXPLORATION

(1500–1700s)

Between the 1500s and 1700s, European countries such as Spain, Portugal, and England set sail in search of new land and riches. The era of discovery may sound exciting, but many lost their lives in the name of exploration.

To reach North and South America, or the "New World," European explorers spent two to three months crossing the Pacific Ocean. Aboard the ships, living quarters were cramped, dirty, and uncomfortable. The food was tightly **rationed**. It was not uncommon for passengers to starve to death before reaching land.

Having food onboard made ships appealing to pests like black rats. This kind of rat and the fleas it carried often spread diseases. Some of the diseases could be passed to people through rat bites or feces. The passengers easily became sick.

And what awaited the brave few who set foot on American soil? They faced a harsh, unfamiliar world. Brutal weather, shortages of food and supplies, attacks by native people, and deadly diseases took a devastating toll on explorers.

FACT
Even an explorer's own crewmembers could be dangerous. **Mutiny**, or crew rebellion, was not uncommon.

Many dangers awaited explorers who reached the shores of the New World.

"The movements of the sea upset our heads and stomachs so horribly that we all turned white as ghosts and began to bring up our very souls. The dwellings are so closed in, dark and evil-smelling that they seem more like burial vaults."

—Spanish sailor Eugenio de Salazar, describing conditions on a discovery ship

ration—to limit to prevent running out of something

mutiny—a revolt against the captain of a ship

COLONIAL AMERICA

(1607–1776)

In 1606 three ships sailed from England to Jamestown, Virginia. The passengers' goal was to set up the first permanent **colony**.

Of the 144 men who set sail, 39 died before reaching Jamestown. At the end of the first year, only 35 of the original 144 were alive. Most had died of **malaria** and starvation.

The early colonists often fought with American Indians. Food and shelter were difficult to acquire. The settlers tried to force Indians into giving up food and supplies. This led to many bloody battles.

King Phillip's War was waged between colonists and several northeastern tribes. The war began in 1675. By the spring of 1678, more than 3,000 Indians were killed. Six hundred colonists were also killed and 1,200 of their homes destroyed. The conflict ended shortly after the capture and killing of Metacom, an Indian leader the colonists called "King Phillip."

colony—a territory settled by people from another country and controlled by that country

malaria—a serious disease that people get from mosquito bites; malaria causes high fever, chills, and sometimes death

Colonists' battles with American Indians could have devastating results.

"Our men were destroyed with cruel diseases as swellings, fluxes (dysentery), burning fevers, and by wars and some died suddenly, but for the most part, they died of mere famine."

— George Percy, an Englishman who sailed on the original voyage to settle the Virginia colonies

HOW THE WEST WAS WILD

(1800–1900)

By the 1800s, the eastern states were crowded. Pioneers moved west in search of a better life, but they often found the opposite.

Life on a wagon train was dangerous. A common cause of death was being crushed beneath a wagon's wheels. Other pioneers lost their lives to disease, accidental gunshots, attacks from other settlers, lightning strikes, grassfires, and snakebites.

Five-month trips from Missouri to the west coast were planned to avoid winter weather. Delays caught travelers unprepared for the deep snow and freezing cold. Travelers might run out of supplies, starve, or freeze to death as they headed west across the Rocky Mountains.

Warm weather wasn't any better. Diseases such as malaria were carried by mosquitoes and horseflies. Other diseases pioneers battled included mumps, measles, cholera, tuberculosis, and smallpox.

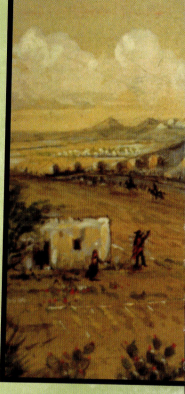

Pioneers headed west in long wagon trains.

Oregon Trail—a pioneer wagon route that led from Missouri to the west coast

FACT

It is estimated that about 20,000 settlers lost their lives traveling the 2,000 miles (3,219 km) along the **Oregon Trail**.

DONNER PARTY DISASTER

The Donner family was part of a group of 87 settlers that left Missouri in 1847. They were headed for California. The wealthy Donners had more comforts in their wagons than most settlers. They left with generous amounts of food, money, beds, and stoves for cooking.

The Donner journey was going well. Then the group tried taking a shortcut through the wintry Sierra Nevada mountains. The group suddenly became trapped.

Snow and bitter cold prevented the Donners from leaving the mountains. Their cattle began to die, and food supplies ran out. Settlers died from exposure, starvation, and sickness. The remaining party members resorted to eating the dead to survive.

It took rescuers many attempts to reach and rescue what was left of the Donner Party. In the end, only 47 of the original 87 settlers survived.

Without an established police force or court system, there was yet another threat to westward travelers: other people.

The violence and dangers increased as the California Gold Rush hit in 1949. Thousands of families left homes in the eastern states to try to strike it rich mining out west. It is estimated that as many as 30 percent of travelers lost their lives.

Like the first trailblazers, these pioneers ran out of food or supplies on the journey. If they reached California, desperate miners faced more difficulties. Many resorted to attacking groups of Indians to gain land and supplies.

By this time, guns were everywhere, and there were no real laws or rules. Legendary robbers such as Jesse James and Billy the Kid were at the height of their game.

If a criminal was caught, the punishment often wasn't decided by a judge and court. Individuals dealt out punishments on their own, and arguments often were settled with violence.

Outlaws rob stagecoach passengers at gunpoint.

MINERS' VIOLENCE

The American Indians who lived in California were described by early explorers as gentle and hard-working. But the miners saw them as weak, disgusting savages. The United States government refused to adopt laws to protect the Indians from miners' attacks. Miners went on "Indian hunts" without ever being punished for their crimes. Thousands of innocent Indians were killed. The miners took their land when they died.

INDUSTRIAL DANGER

(1750–1850)

The Industrial Revolution began in England in the 1750s and spread to Europe and the United States. New machines and coal-powered factories produced goods faster than ever before. Widely-available products improved lives for many. But this was not the case for the factory workers themselves.

Factory workers had no legal protection. Workplaces were often overcrowded and uncomfortable. Temperatures could reach more than 100 degrees Fahrenheit (38 degrees Celsius). Employees worked 12-hour shifts and rarely were allowed breaks.

Factory machines had powerful turning gears. With no barrier to separate workers from the gears, it was not uncommon for workers to lose a hand or an arm in the machines.

Although factory jobs were dangerous, poor workers needed the money. As time went on, more and more people moved to the city looking for jobs. If a worker complained about conditions or got hurt on the job, he or she could be easily replaced.

Child workers were common during the Industrial Revolution.

THE DANGEROUS LIVES OF CHILDREN

In Great Britain children made up a large part of the labor force during the Industrial Revolution. Children as young as 4 years old worked long hours for very little money. In England, 40 percent of the workers in the cotton mills were under 18. In some areas, 18 percent of the workers were 9 years old or younger. Children were so small many had to stand on crates to be able to reach the machines.

With factories running at full force, the need for coal increased. As demand rose, mines were dug deeper and deeper. In the depths of the coal mines, workers encountered poisonous and explosive natural gases. Without a vent system to pump in fresh air, these gases could be deadly.

Other mining dangers included falling down mine shafts, being crushed by cave-ins, and being run over by coal carts.

The dust created from cutting and handling coal was yet another problem. Breathing in the dangerous dust made miners sick with black lung. Also called miner's cough, in severe cases this sickness led to heart failure and even death.

But miners weren't the only people affected by the dangers of coal. Coal dug in the mines was burned to create energy for factories. The factories released a thick coal smoke that filled the air. Coal dust and smoke was nearly unavoidable.

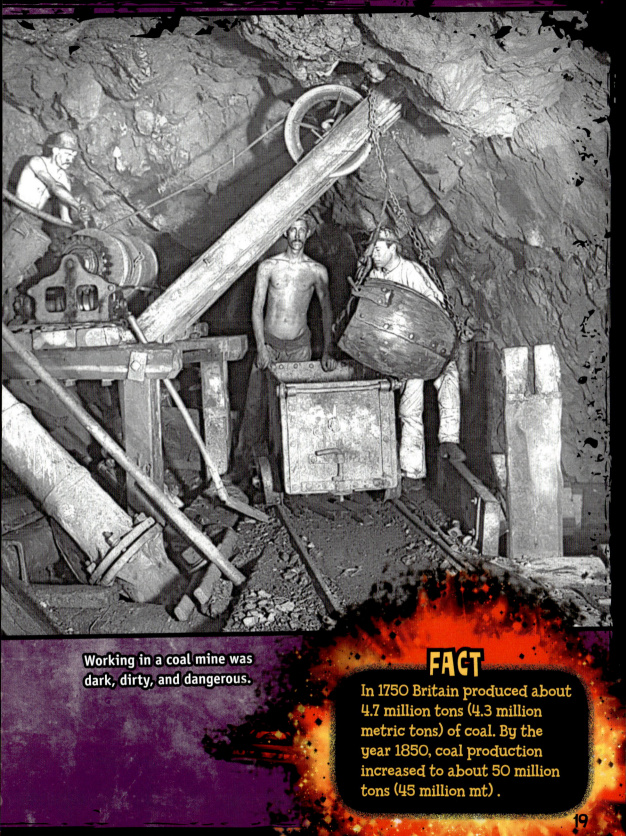

Working in a coal mine was dark, dirty, and dangerous.

FACT

In 1750 Britain produced about 4.7 million tons (4.3 million metric tons) of coal. By the year 1850, coal production increased to about 50 million tons (45 million mt).

DEATH IN THE GREAT DEPRESSION

(1930-1940s)

In 1929 the United States suffered a financial disaster that led to what is known as the Great Depression. Across the country businesses closed. By 1934, 25 out of 100 American workers were unemployed. People couldn't afford to pay for their houses and many became homeless. Families couldn't afford to buy food, and people often went days without eating.

Those without jobs would go to common areas in the city to find work as day laborers. There were often only a few jobs, and people were trampled and beaten as they fought to get work.

Homeless families gathered in dangerous **shantytowns**. Garbage rotted in the streets, attracting disease-carrying rats. There were no outhouses or plumbing, and human waste was left on the streets. Rivers of human waste seeped into the water people drank and made them very sick. People were often beaten and killed in fights over food.

a 1930s shantytown

shantytown—an area of a city where there are many shacks and often no running water or electricity

THE COLD WAR AND FEAR

(1947-1991)

Millions have died in wars fought over land and power. During the Cold War, nuclear weapons took the fear of war to the next level.

After World War II (1939-1945), the democratic United States and the **communist** Soviet Union were fierce opponents. Both countries built **atomic bombs** and pointed them at each other. It seemed only a matter of time before nuclear war would erupt. People feared the worst.

Consider the damage caused by a single large nuclear bomb dropped in the center of a major city. Anyone standing within 1 mile (1.6 km) of a bomb site would be instantly vaporized in the explosion's fireball. Anyone who survived within 5 miles (8 km) of the blast would die of radiation poisoning and severe burns in less than two weeks.

---

communist—practicing communism, a political system in which there is no private property and everything is owned and shared

atomic bomb—a powerful bomb that explodes with great force

A nuclear bomb explosion creates a fiery mushroom cloud.

"I made one great mistake in my life when I signed the letter to President Roosevelt recommending that atom bombs be made ..."

—Professor Albert Einstein

Today students have fire and severe weather drills in school. During the Cold War, they also had nuclear raid drills. Schools prepared students for what to do if an atomic bomb was launched.

The terror of the Cold War era led many Americans to build fallout shelters in their backyards. These underground shelters were designed to protect occupants from nuclear fallout for two weeks. In that time the debris from a nuclear blast will decay enough for people to safely return aboveground.

Fallout shelters included the basic supplies needed to survive for two weeks. They contained nonperishable food, water, oil lamps, medical supplies, prescriptions, and equipment to monitor outside conditions.

COUNTRIES WITH NUCLEAR CAPABILITIES	
COUNTRY	YEAR FIRST BOMB WAS MADE
United States	1945
Russian Federation, formerly the Soviet Union	1949
United Kingdom	1952
France	1960
China	1964
India	1979
Pakistan	1998
North Korea	2009

Young students participate in a nuclear raid drill.

FACT

In the 1990s, the country of South Africa became the first to dismantle all its nuclear weapons in the name of peace.

Danger in the 21st Century

2001-PRESENT

On September 11, 2001, terrorists hijacked U.S. airliners and crashed them into the Pentagon and World Trade Center. Since then, the United States and other governments have stepped up efforts to stop acts of terrorism.

Because of its violent nature, terrorism has been on the mind of the public. While acts of terrorism claim thousands of lives, there is an even bigger threat that affects many more people.

Today dangers faced by millions of people around the world are poverty and the lack of basic necessities. More than 700 million people do not have a clean, safe source of water. The World Health Organization reports that every year, around 2 million people die because of unsafe water and poor sanitation and hygiene.

Worldwide, starvation claims millions of lives every year. It takes the heaviest toll in the poorest parts of the world, such as Africa and India. In 2011 it is estimated that 6 million children died worldwide from **malnutrition**.

malnutrition—condition caused by a lack of healthful foods in the diet

Human aid organizations supply fresh water to the people of Andes Mtito, Kenya, Africa.

"Water has become a highly precious resource. There are some places where a barrel of water costs more than a barrel of oil."

—Lloyd Axworthy, Foreign Minister of Canada

Some threats haven't changed much over hundreds of years. Both now and then, natural disasters, war, and disease kill millions of people. Technology, modern medicine, and stronger security help, but there will always be dangers to human life.

Today you may not have to worry about dying while traveling in a wagon train. But as times change, so do the threats humans face. The most dangerous era might be yet to come.

TIMELINE OF DANGEROUS ERAS

1348-1400
The Black Death pandemic strikes Europe, Asia, and North America.

1675-1678
More than 3,000 American Indians and 600 colonists die in King Phillip's War.

1492
Christopher Columbus sets sail for the New World.

1847
The 87 members of the Donner Party depart from Missouri. Only 47 survive.

1947–1991
The Cold War begins after World War II ends. The United States and Russia race to build nuclear weapons.

1934
The Great Depression, which began in 1929, causes the unemployment rate to soar to 25 percent.

1849–1859
Thousands of people travel west from the eastern United States to search for gold in California.

1850
Great Britain produces about 50 million tons (45 million mt) of coal to fuel the country's Industrial Revolution.

2001
On September 11, nearly 3,000 people die when terrorists hijack and crash four U.S. planes.

GLOSSARY

atomic bomb (uh-TOM-ik BOM)—a powerful bomb that explodes with great force; atomic bombs destroy large areas and leave behind dangerous radiation

boil (BOYL)—a painful, swollen spot on the body that is usually caused by an infection

bubonic plague (boo-BAW-nick PLAYG)—a fatal disease with painful swelling of the lymph glands and a darkening of the skin

colony (KAH-luh-nee)—a territory settled by people from another country and controlled by that country

communist (KAHM-yuh-nist)—country or person practicing communism, a political system in which there is no private property and everything is shared

malaria (muh-LAIR-ee-ah)—a serious disease that people get from mosquito bites

malnutrition (mal-noo-TRISH-uhn)—condition caused by a lack of healthful foods in the diet

mutiny (MYOOT-uh-nee)—a revolt against the captain of a ship

Oregon Trail (AWR-uh-gun TRAYL)—a pioneer wagon route that led from Missouri to the west coast

ration (RASH-uhn)—to limit to prevent running out of something

shantytown (SHAN-tee-town)—an area of a city where there are many shacks and sometimes no running water or electricity

terrorist (TER-ur-ist)—someone who uses violence and threats to frighten or harm people and to achieve a politcal or religious goal

vaccination (vak-suh-NAY-shun)—a shot of medicine that protects people from a disease

READ MORE

Asselin, Kristine Carlson. *The Real Story on the Weapons and Battles of Colonial America.* Life in the American Colonies. Mankato, Minn.: Capstone Press, 2012.

Park, Louise. *Life in the Middle Ages.* Ancient Civilizations. New York: PowerKids Press, 2013.

Keller, Susanna. *The True Story of Christopher Columbus.* What Really Happened. New York: PowerKids Press, 2013.

INTERNET SITES

FactHound offers a safe, fun way to find Internet sites related to this book. All of the sites on FactHound have been researched by our staff.

Here's all you do:

Visit www.facthound.com

Type in this code: 9781476501260

Check out projects, games and lots more at
www.capstonekids.com

INDEX

Billy the Kid, 14
black plague, 4
bubonic plague, 6, 7

California Gold Rush, 14, 29
child workers, 17
coal, 4, 16, 18, 19, 29
Cold War, 22, 24, 29
colonists, 10
Columbus, Christopher, 28
Crusades, 6

disease, 4, 6, 8, 10, 12, 20, 28
Donner Party, 13, 28

factories, 16, 18
food, 8, 10, 13, 14, 20, 24

Great Depression, 20, 29

Industrial Revolution, 16, 29

James, Jesse, 14

King Phillip, 10, 28

medicine, 4, 28
Middle Ages, 6
mutiny, 9

natural disasters, 12
nuclear weapons, 22, 24, 29

Oregon Trail, 13

Pentagon, 26
pioneers, 12, 14

rats, 7, 8, 20

settlers, 10, 12, 13
shantytowns, 20
supplies, 8, 10, 12, 13, 14, 24

terrorists, 4, 26, 29

water, 26
weather, 8, 12, 24
World Health Organization, 26
World Trade Center, 26
World War II, 22, 29